AUTOMOTIVE

poems by

Ceridwen Hall

Finishing Line Press
Georgetown, Kentucky

AUTOMOTIVE

Copyright © 2020 by Ceridwen Hall
ISBN 978-1-64662-381-5 First Edition
All rights reserved under International and Pan-American Copyright Conventions. No part of this book may be reproduced in any manner whatsoever without written permission from the publisher, except in the case of brief quotations embodied in critical articles and reviews.

ACKNOWLEDGMENTS

Grateful acknowledgement is made to editors of the following journals in which these poems or versions of these poems appeared:

Cold Mountain Review: "Evidence"
Poet Lore: "Commute"
Prairie Fire: "Vehicular Metaphor"
Tar River Poetry: "at the DMV"
Rattle: "Changing the License Plates"
Harpur Palate: "Incident"
riverSedge: "Interstate"
Antiphon: "Compliment"
The Moth: "Jellyfish"
Speckled Trout Review: "Return"
Cloudbank: "30 degrees" and "Moving across the Midwest"

Publisher: Leah Maines
Editor: Christen Kincaid
Cover Art: Photo by Martin Kallur on Unsplash
Author Photo: Alanah Hall
Cover Design: Elizabeth Maines McCleavy

Order online: www.finishinglinepress.com
also available on amazon.com

Author inquiries and mail orders:
Finishing Line Press
P. O. Box 1626
Georgetown, Kentucky 40324
U. S. A.

Table of Contents

Self : Driving 1

at the DMV 2

30 Degrees 3

The Fisherwoman 4

Evidence 5

Surface 7

Visibility 8

Compliment 9

Incident 10

Commute 11

Jellyfish 12

Ars Poetica with Engine Trouble 13

Mountain Passage 14

Interstate 15

Changing the License Plates 16

Moving Across the Midwest 18

Vehicular Metaphor 19

Return 21

For my mother—bold explorer and wise navigator

Self : Driving

I cross Indiana, northward and west. Green sharpens some pastures; others are mud. My thoughts stretch linear, then they scatter. Clouds waver and gleam on the faces of ponds. Watching the new calves' shivering walk reflected, I consider the promise of driverless cars. Untether a threat. Absent need to steer, would I tend—and to what? Automobile already means self-moving. If a trance arises between hesitations—momentum suspends me— errors remain possible, and decisions.

at the DMV

you go sweet and pliant
for convenience sake, let
the clerk decide your eyes
are blue like the many chairs
and the number 41 you are
assigned

to be processed; you wait and stand
and answer yes and no and 1987
and recite the letters in the vision
screening; something peripheral
flashes and you lift an arm, consent
to be an organ donor; 5'7, then spell
your entire name again

until it sounds strange to you
and like the surface of water, ripples
or splashes; when you sign the registry,
you find you've been labeled male,
point the error out, nicely, are asked
to repeat your data, watch all of it

bob around as if in a blue pool
where letters grow light and plastic
and the weather is lovely today
you agree and write a check,
then sit at the monitor and answer
questions about fog or how to pass
slower vehicles, how to survive

various abstract and hypothetical
scenarios on roads unlike any
you've driven in this state
or ever—but you press buttons
in the correct sequence, proceed
to be photographed, gaze straight,
as directed, at the butterfly icon

30 Degrees

Snow dusts the concrete at dawn,
not cumulative, just obscuring
patches of ice. I brush the windshield,
ignore the roof. Every few winters
this self starts to feel like a pretense.
Why name and face difficulty
in a body, in thought. It thrashes
or goes still when you fail to recognize
that gaze in the rearview. A warning:
she rejects every available friction,
sways rudderless. A stranger in pajamas
stops me to ask for money and prayers,
but this 'I' seems unable to meet any need,
unable to speak even. Blame arrives,
then guilt. It takes so long to heat the car
each time. And what's autonomy—
a series of decisions. Hours and clouds
shift. Steam rises. Vessels constrict
in this weather; blood abandons
extremities. I want, idly, to be more
kind, more anything. Crystals of salt
encrust the road and every passing tire.

The Fisherwoman

My mother drives to the airport. I sit behind
my father, with their luggage pile. We speak

little—of unseasonable weather and the new
police station under construction on a corner

near the freeway entrance—and watch mist
drift off the Ohio in little rags. We leave

our city and pass into the surrounding hills
and pastures. Then we circle the airport.

When we reach a line for departing flights,
my mother waits until she can maneuver us

parallel to the curb, where I'll be able to pull
smoothly back into traffic—rehearsing

inversion; I unload their gear. Rain begins
splotching the walkway. They go. I tilt

the seat by hand, a fraction, and turn the key.

Evidence

The car was probably used in a crime
and dumped in the river, my mother told us
years later. It was my sister's car—she drove
us to school most days. But the morning
we discovered the absence of the car
was a Saturday or during vacation.
We were going instead to run errands
and I was sent out to unlock the car
ahead of my mother and younger siblings.
But the car was not where we'd left it
the previous afternoon. I'd walked out
the back door and around the house
to notice this disappearance. Now I ran
straight across the lawn to tell my mother,
who did not believe me at first. As a child
I never lied, but was prone to overstatement.
I gave back the keys and we all went outside.
The car was not there. My mother wondered
if it had rolled downhill, if we'd mistaken
where the car was supposed to be. We went
up and down the block. Most likely, I held
my sister's hand while my mother carried
our brother on her left hip. Their seats
were strapped in the missing car. Stolen,
my mother decided. She called the police
from the kitchen, called my sister (away,
I think, visiting her mother.) An officer came
out to take a statement from us. He wanted
to hear which Winnie-the-Poo sticker rested
on each window when he learned my sister
had put them up to entertain us. I was called
from the play-set because my mother didn't know;

I recited where each of us sat, which character
sat beside each of us. I remember speaking
to this man who'd brought his gun and car
to our driveway (without sirens), remember
craning my neck to look up at him because
he did not crouch down the way cops do
when they speak to children on television.
He carried a clipboard and wrote in pencil.
But I no longer know what I told him (other
than that I had the front seat because
I was oldest). I wasn't afraid of him,
but of his authority. Perhaps I already knew
that the car was irretrievable. He nodded,
I was sent away. The police explained odds
were against their finding the car; overnight,
thieves would have ditched the evidence.
My sister replaced it in August. I began
to see how impermanent our childhood
fixtures. The car wasn't ever found
and must have sunk, rusted. I remember
it smelling of coffee, think it belonged
first to our father and then to my sister,
and sometimes I imagine water filling
it, dissolving those stickers. The river
was only a few miles from our house,
but the current would have taken the car
farther downstream, to be dredged
and scrapped.

surface

I vehicle and drift—the usual error—out for groceries; a yellow light demands rapid [but this reckless is mostly systemic—or carbon, and we collude] wheeling left— through traffic—to park; shop, exit

through automatic doors

step by instinct toward my previous model—remember a sudden freeze and sliding downhill, being unable to stop before impact: airbags, repairs, etc.; for years after, I drove cautiously—but dreamed of veering toward bodies of water—until rain flooded the streets and filled my engine

                                        [insurance declared weather]

then I went pedestrian, while oceanside

so I remain in the habit of moving and thinking; worry at crosswalks, what I am capable of forgetting, worry, backing—mind chiming between rear camera lines

                                            and figures, wandering

Visibility

        An empty bottle rotates in the wind ahead,

then in the mirror. I too am strange

        to all my previous selves, despite history,

despite patterns entrenched. Fences slip by

        outside and I mistake animals for symbols:

a crow eats road kill, two horses drink

        from a small pond. The grass is faded brown,

but I try to mark where the fields end,

        where the hills first lift. There's nothing exact

about transformation. Landmarks arise,

        blur into memory; I will be again, surrounded

by the people who know me now because

        they knew me once. A slow river doubles

the bridge—with pillars stretched across water.

Compliment

Biking with you is like biking alone,
but knowing someone will be along
if I crash, my sister tells me. Because going
downhill, I brake non-stop, unwilling
to approach the velocity of thought. I worry
I might ruin my brakes trying to control
each descent, but fear wins out. She waits
for me or makes a small loop. We're going
to argue later. I'm letting her decide for now
which way to turn because this frees me
to consider (I should mention the cemetery
paths are empty, the engraved names legible
in passing) how, unlike a car, a bicycle
exposes us to the elements. How our hands
both stop and steer. Obvious notions,
but enough for now. It's refreshing to depart
the usual metaphors, the usual problem. Mortality
isn't abstract here, but like the geese near
the pond. You approach and then steer around
when they refuse to budge. I suspect joy
and sorrow are analogous in that both can be
distinguished from pleasure. Here we are
in the city and also not. We used to visit
as children to feed breadcrumbs to the ducks.
When you are young, nothing is odd. But I was
a nervous child. It took three adults all spring
to teach me to bicycle. I wanted very much
for balance and momentum to be separate
ideas, for time not to be involved with either.
I've since grown into my anxiety. Circling
the dead, these memories seem inevitable.
Our argument also. When my sister turns
up a steep hill, I choose not to follow, make
another loop around the pond. Having no pride,
we agreed earlier, means almost the same thing
as having no shame, though I won't think this
when we argue. Overhead, an eagle lands
on a branch; I step aside and wait.

Incident

What's unexpected becomes event and pivot
of a day. They were discussing political unrest

on the radio, and bombings. Because the sound
registered first, I wondered—in brief animal

startlement—was that deliberate, for effect?
Then the bump reverberated: fact: stillness,

though 'rear-ended' would elude me until
I no longer required an explanation. I told

the agent I'd been hit from behind. True,
sloppy language. She said I wasn't at fault.

But I should have left earlier to avoid traffic.
Or I might have taken another route, refused

my sister's request for a visit. Violence abrupts
distance; circumstance, intent. And to think

I'd worried for years about left turns, children
chasing toys. But rarely this, despite warnings

against hesitation and slow driving. Adrenaline
is meant to keep the body running, but no one

was hurt. Only shaken. We exchanged numbers
and photographed licenses as scientists named

selves our neural tendency to repeat or narrate
pathways. Signaled over a violin sonata, merged

between two crawling trucks.

Commute

You pause an extra beat at the four-way stop. It's dark
and the rain is light; you barely need windshield wipers.

On the radio: a song you haven't heard in ten years.
Soon you'll turn, park facing the building you live in

now and shut off the engine and be alone and know
you are—contemplating the short walk across

the lot, upstairs to your numbered door, non-descript
rooms. It might take longer than usual to find your key

—the car's engine will cease whirring and grow
silent. You will think of what you need to bring

inside, what you should do next. You realize
there's no avoiding this moment, its brief inertia,

but you drive more slowly. The wipers' metronome
for your thoughts is almost company, and to walk

inside will require no effort—steps lifting the mind
like a sleeping child. But first the moment of sitting

alone at the wheel, knowing a day has passed.

Jellyfish

Arrival is also a departure. The wind lifts
a flag like any other fabric, ripples it. I am
so distracted by change, by the cold sunset.
Because my sister is driving, I see geese
land in pairs. They are sleek and fat, drink
from a fountain dividing the road. I'm afraid
to want anything right now, visiting family.
With memory, sometimes years grow wild
and their details obscure. We cross the lot,
one so ordinary it reminds us of hundreds
of other lots. After dinner, we return to the car
and our conversation about dreams, which recur
but are distorted in the telling. I'd forgotten that
if you lay down across the middle seat, all you see
are the silhouettes of trees, how you might be
anywhere. But, nearer, you can hear more deeply
the rumble of tires. I sit upright again and notice
someone drawing curtains. For her, we are two beads
of light moving along a row, anonymous. We reach
our street and I turn my head to study the houses
whose rooms, like jellyfish, glow unknowable.

Ars Poetica with Engine Trouble

the faraway city summons—you turn
a hurried key, mind already halved, and
nothingness follows, a low grind, static-
strewn, then the ominous chime; you think
of warranties, of batteries, how you meant
to clear the fine layer of dust from the altar
of the dash; but the city insists—you try
again: the engine balks, the brain rattles

you press a hand to where the sunroof
would be, study the dome of the car's skull,
and conjure a patch of road, a winding hazard,
which beckons, through pastures and mountains,
with lengths of yellow paint; wind draws stray
plastics and sage into your path; hesitant,
you remember previous accidents, measure
potential harm; but the city is not patient;
its decision drops like an egg: between you
many rivers demand crossing

so you listen for a soft click, you walk
around the car and inspect tires; your feet
now whisper the city's name; suspecting
the compartment manual will be useless,
you think instead of your mother, who talks
to chickens as she roasts them—nonsense
about herbs and seasons—and yet it works;
you check the gears, fidget the steering column
into better alignment, but your throat hollows

when you most want to speak—you watch
instead, as if night fog had swallowed
the road, left you scrying the gulf for beams
from your own headlights, carving
one slow mile, carving another

Mountain Passage

Combing the windblown snow for road, I cease
to think of the orange and red squares claiming

to monitor danger. The current runs colorless
and tidal over painted lines. I follow a truck's

taillights—just visible at safe distance—until
endless levels off. During a week of predicted

hazards, I forswore travel, then today, decided,
despite the weather, I must go. On this journey

I am not myself; I am some capable madwoman.
Signs read: Turn off cruise control. They measure

gusts in miles per hour. The trucks' brakes whine
like animals searching for the lost; wind answers.

Listening, we bend, half-blind, into sweeping bright.

Interstate

Billboards loom near Platte, Nebraska, and the clouds threaten
more snow, maybe hail. I accelerate and coast, adjust and adjust
the heat. Exits drift farther apart; I-80 empties into a paved river.
My eyes follow it or visit the screen that tracks accumulating miles
and exterior temperature. In theory, this computer will stop the car
for any detected obstacle; meanwhile, wind presses leftward,
north. Do I trust this? No, but thought narrows, slips its ruminants
—a relief: not to be separate from, not to search beyond, the road.
It appears ahead, then is swallowed. The brakes wait underfoot,
the wheel rests level in my grip. As if to confuse reverence
and weariness, the dog sleeps to low music. Navigation tells
us to keep left, then falls silent.

Changing the License Plates

You have put off this task for weeks—for lack
of time, for lack of tools—but now you kneel

behind the car you've driven for twelve years,
since high school. You aren't sure anymore

exactly what your life is supposed to resemble.
But it's probably illegal to continue driving

with out-of-state plates attached and in-state
plates left sealed in plastic on the front seat

and today might be the last warm afternoon
in October. So you've borrowed a wrench

and screw-driver from your landlord's shed
and, one by one, you loosen the old screws,

then lay them in a row across the bumper.
You don't use tools often, but your hands

seem to remember what to do. You pull
the old plate free and study it: a number

you never bothered to memorize, a stack
of renewal decals with your mother's date

of birth. You still don't think of this car
as belonging to you. What does it mean,

anyway, to own a vehicle, to maintain it?
Your fingers appear strange and liable

as they lower this plate to the ground, fit
the new one in place. You decide to store

the old plate in the trunk like a corpse
or a kit for emergencies. Then you walk

to the front plate, where a bolt proves
difficult. Loose hair falls across your face,

but your hands are grimy, so you ignore it.
You secure the plate, consider the slogan:

Land of Lincoln, which seems level enough
for your purposes—for whoever it is you are

impersonating or becoming. The dog watches
from the window as you test the plates to see

if they wiggle. Not much. You stand and lock
the doors, go to return what you've borrowed.

Moving Across the Midwest

      I'm speeding for once; I'm trying to believe
in calculated risk, that a danger you can measure
doesn't belong to you anymore. I race my own
weariness to stay alert on this familiar path:
music, caffeine. Dusk stretches long and transient,
then thickens. I don't rein my mind's wandering
stride—why should I? Monotony threatens worse
—creep of the surreal assumption this is endless
until I forget I am mortal. Anger is a one way
to keep awake, uncertainty another. Any chasm
to brace against, to bridge. When the sky is dark,
only cities seem to exist—or cities only seem to exist
at night. Then the occasional tree, leaves silvered
in headlights. And the sudden possum. I swerve,
flinch, as if I am the one who would be crushed.
You inherited my anxious brain, Dad said yesterday,
the unintuitive wiring. I argued: we're all intuitive,
it's just that some reflexes are more adaptive than
others. The shoulder narrows. I shouldn't drift
near these trucks, but it was a revelation to see
the rooms emptied; how easy it is to abandon a life,
how interchangeable every open space. Hundreds
of orange barrels gleam and vanish.

Vehicular Metaphor

No, we aren't there yet. There is more existential

even than death. It's dark just now, but we know
we haven't arrived. The headlights show us only

pieces of the road ahead. We take it in turns to drive.

Sometimes we stop for supplies or to make repairs,
if repairs are possible. Then we climb back inside

and continue. Because this car is old, our siblings

are the only safety features. They are here in case
of parental error. Or in case the parents didn't err

enough. The road seems to go on forever. We don't

believe this to be true. At some point, it must end
in a gravel lot. Or we will come to a definitive turn.

We think we'll know it when we see it, but aren't sure

exactly what it is or when when might be. Our father
has told us he'll let us know once he reaches the age

where he can stop eating gummy bears before he gets

queasy. It's like that, we think, but without the bright
shapes. So we think it may be far away. We may need

to stop and walk in separate directions. If the car flips

it could hurl us into the night. The engine isn't quiet
necessarily, but we are accustomed to the sound of it

and the roll of the tires. Sometimes we talk, but not

always, about other roads, the oddness of our being
on this one, which for now runs parallel to a creek

and a wide field beyond which we cannot yet see.

Return

I go back expecting to be glad: all the fields

green, sudden, the trees edged with buds. And yet.

My brain is a reluctant vessel. It watches the near sky,

sees its white mirror in a flooded ditch. Metamorphosis

entails loss. I note the lonely horse, the circling hawk.

We tell ourselves weather is scenery, not dream,

but the rain says otherwise. Even brief joy weighs us

to the road, the hour before dusk—living, hurtling,

becomes necessary. Rivulets, meanwhile, stream

across the windshield, run earthward.

Additional Acknowledgements

I am indebted to the creative writing communities at the University of Illinois, Urbana-Champaign and the University of Utah for their help in revising these poems.

Thank you to Janice Harrington, Jessica Rae Bergamino, and Paula Mendoza for your kind words at the finish of this project.

I am so grateful to my parents, who are always ready to welcome me home or to wave me off on my next journey. And to my siblings, who shared the back seat with me through many adventures.

Ceridwen Hall is a poet, editor, and teacher from Cincinnati, Ohio. Although she's lived on both coasts and in the mountains, she retains a deep appreciation for the Midwest and its roads.

She completed her MFA at the University of Illinois, Urbana-Champaign, and her PhD at the University of Utah, where she received the Clarence Snow Fellowship and the Levis Prize in Poetry. Her poems and essays have appeared in *Spoon River Poetry Review, TriQuarterly, Pembroke Magazine, Tar River Poetry, The Cincinnati Review*, and other journals.

www.ingramcontent.com/pod-product-compliance
Lightning Source LLC
LaVergne TN
LVHW041521070426
835507LV00012B/1734